WORD WEAVING

Lois York

For Barbara
Love,
Lois

BAMBAZ Press
Los Angeles 2016

Interior Artwork: Lois York
Cover Artwork: Lois York
Photo of Author: Baz Here
Book Design: Baz Here
Editor: Bambi Here

BAMBAZ Press
548 S. Spring Street
Suite 1201
Los Angeles, CA 90013
contact: bambi@bambazpress.com

ISBN: 978-1-365-15191-0
Printed in the United States of America

I need words to go forward.

–Paul Kanalithi
from *When Breath Becomes Air*

In memory of Peaches N. Cream

TABLE OF CONTENTS

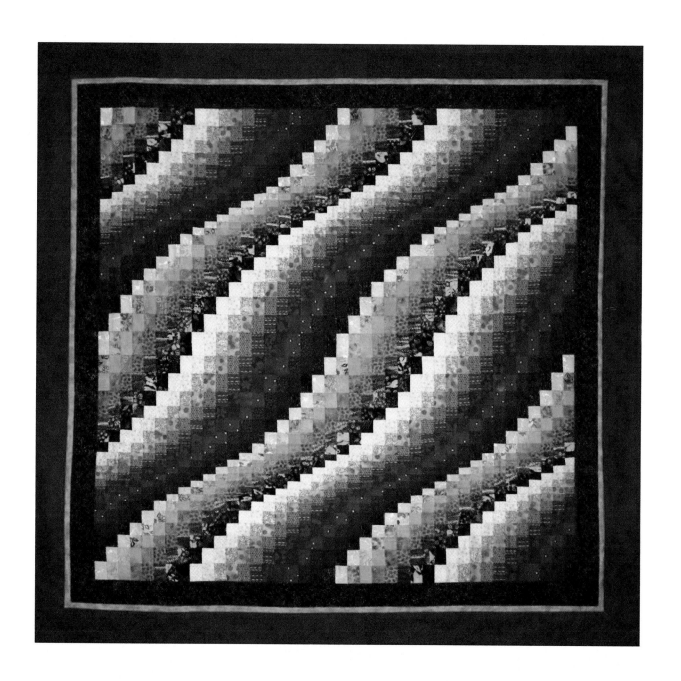

Beach Music

EUPHORIA

Color melts into my blood.
The window is a frame for mountains crayoned into the sky.
I see that blue and want it to be the handle of reality—
or something bigger than life.
The trees appear with priestly dress, their ears waiting.
How did the brokenness become smooth?

The media tells fairy tales—
unlimited access to information that is faulty.
We are flies on the bottle of disease.
Women over 80 are afraid.
Stampeding bulls outrace taxis.
Some people believe we can save the earth.
Fabrics feel delicious in my hands.
Euphoria is the exploration of color.

THE GALAXY IS A HAPPENING THING

Sitting at the edge of the Pacific Ocean, I feel like I own the world. I am just here to oversee it. I count the sandpipers running in the wet surf, finding hors d'oeuvres among the grains of sand. The lone sailboat lists in the wind while clouds hang in frosting layers close to the horizon. I can see the pier and Palos Verdes and just a hint of Catalina. The dolphins are playing their underwater games so I can't see them. Silver. Silver is the color of the top of the water. Waves are timid, waiting for the currents to change. I see a jet soaring off to someplace west of here. A woman walks, a woman stands in the water, a woman sits with her laptop. Oh, that one is me. But my eyes are all-encompassing today. I see far. I understand something about depth today. There is something I cannot get from people. Something that communion with nature provides me.

The woman walking approaches me. I am usually cautious about such things on the beach, but she is smiling, very thin, and I can see streaks of gray in her shoulder-length hair. She is wearing a warm-up suit and running shoes. She says hello and we start a conversation. "Sorry to interrupt your work," she says. "It's not really work, I'm writing a book." "Thought maybe you were."

After getting through why we were on the beach, nearly alone on such a cloudy day, and why I looked so cheerful today, and why she was feeling so sad, we felt like we had been long-time friends. Her husband of 40 years had left her two weeks ago to move in with his girlfriend. She was left in a beach-front, high-rise apartment. What attracted her to me was that she felt my cheerfulness. I felt her deep sorrow.

We exchanged email addresses and I said I knew she would enjoy reading my book. After trying to figure out how she was going to pay me the $20 and I was going to deliver the book, I said, "Walk with me to my car and I'll give you a book." Which we did. Then she hugged me and said, "You were just the angel I needed to meet today." So, I drove home with a little spark in my heart. Just being alive seems enough. The galaxy is a happening thing.

BLAME THE ROSE PARADE

We can blame the Rose Parade.
The flowers, the bare shoulders,
the sun hats on TV in January
entice pilgrimages.

People eagerly leave brutal weather behind:
ice headaches, frozen nostrils,
car batteries plugged in
to ensure a re-start.
They leave gray skies,
drizzle,
chest colds,
ice-broken electric lines,
burst water pipes,
black-ice roads,
salt-damaged cars.

They leave light-deprived
suicidal thoughts,
snow shovels,
windshield scrapers,
soaring heating bills,
school closures.

They jet to the place
of eternal summer,
find stress-less
beaches and golf courses,
farmers markets and
outdoor dining.
They decide to stay.
Perhaps to find peace,
spirituality, their mojo.

California seems the answer to
stressed marriages,
asthmatic children,
vitamin D deficiencies,
seasonal adjustments.
We melt into California.
It becomes ours.

News stations broadcast
boring weather reports
Then hot, worrisome weather reports,
advice on water conservation,
fines for water overuse,
fear of financial failure,
food shortage,
thirst.

Now we long for cloudy days,
rumbling thunder,
flashes of lightning.
We long for the smell
of dust descending
before the rain
comes down to wash us.

Soon we may leave
California, pack up,
for lack of
inclement weather.

THE EDGE OF WATER

I ran to the edge of the lake
sharp roots poked my native feet.
The sand was mostly under water,
shells, tiny and similar,
stones more beautiful in the water
than dry in the sun.
The reeds could be pulled into small
sections and put together again
like building toys.

A snake might appear
in the grass behind me
and scare me,
but not as much as the surprising
jump of a frog.
The water was warm in the heat of July.
Staying in it, or even under it,
hidden all day
until my lips turned blue
or the sun went down was safest.

Fall came and the lake was coated
with golden pollen
forbidden to touch.
It caused swimmer's itch.

Winter covered all with ice and snow.
If a strong wind came
before the lake was solid,
it sprayed the grasses, twigs,
and maybe even the snakes
into magical ice art,
prisms for sun rays,
making crystals of my summer.

THE ROCK

I stubbed my toe in the surf
of the blue, blue Mediterranean Sea.
I reached down and picked up
a rock, shaped like a heart
as big as my hand.
Very porous,
multi-colored, the solid parts are probably granite.
Heavy, like a pound of butter.
The best part is its shape—
definitely a heart rock.
My collection awaits it.

I packed it at the bottom of my carry-on,
and lugged it, forgotten, through southern Spain.
At the airport
the red light flashed at the x-ray machine.
Three security officers
surrounded me
while one dug through my bag.
Was I stealing Spanish real estate?
Was I hiding drugs in the tiny holes?

I convinced them it was for my collection
of heart rocks
from every country.
They sighed, shook their heads,
and let me keep it.
Now, on my windowsill,
my heart rock reminds me
of falling in love with cerulean blue,
guitar music, sangria,
and Spain.

l stole a Spanish heart

and escaped.
It's only fair
to take a heart with me
while leaving
some of my own behind.

WRITTEN ACROSS THE SKY

You remember the search,
the transition of life.
(It happens in your 40s.)
From a thread of DNA.
From a longing for better.
From a new awareness.
From the feeling that you have
done all you can from this vantage point,
and unless you choose
what is next,
you will die.

Imbedded in the frost on
the winter window,
stuck between the screen
and the outdoors,
I will wait until
spring comes again
and I wonder what it was
I wanted to do.

You'll wonder
what you were thinking
at the time.
You'll wish you had made
a decision
or a choice
or at least a shot in the dark—
like wearing shorts more often
and less makeup.

I am pulled along
the road winding toward
and between the lakes,

deep bodies of water
with answers.

Clouds writing my name
over and over,
lead me in the direction of
my blindness.

I leap in silence
from an un-porous rock,
through the clean air,
plunging into cold, deep,
water.
Going under
to touch bottom
just to see if it is there.

Neighborhoods

BROKEN SIDEWALKS

She paces the sidewalk,
phone to her ear.
Her voice rises, then lowers.
She pleads, then listens.

I saw her earlier,
sitting on the sidewalk,
shoulders down.
I was about to go comfort her,
but she turned and I saw her phone
pressed to her ear—
the picture of sadness, anxiety,
fury, hopelessness.
It's called divorce in the making.

Two small boys who need two parents
wait indoors, overhearing her,
their future at stake.
My heart goes out to her,
she could learn
from my experience.
But no one walks down
the broken sidewalks of divorce
the same way.

INVISIBLE HOUSE

The house is gone, but the view is still there—
the Red River, flowing north, green lawns,
tall grasses, a bike path, jungle gym.
Bulldozed to make space for a dike
to protect the flood plain.
I had left it, now it had left me.

I stood where the front entry had been,
imagined I saw my children, one chasing another
down the hallway.
I stepped forward into the living room and
heard the piano playing "Maple Leaf Rag."
Could he give it a break already?

The dining room was holding laughter
from the dinner party for someone's birthday,
coffee still warm in half-empty cups.
I avoided the bedroom with its
whispered arguments, icy silences.
Well, wouldn't you?

I once lived on the banks of the Red River,
beautiful,
but sometimes dangerous,
bearing thin ice and cold, murky water.
I would often escape to the winter's
snow-covered ski paths, purple at twilight.
Or, in summer, walk along the banks
where red-winged black birds sang their
hopeful songs among the grasses.

I pictured bikes strewn on the lawn,
even the red one that was stolen later.
Children's voices rang at high pitches.

I smelled their sweaty hair as they ran past me
while I stood in the rose garden—
that I was never promised, but got.

Now, only the air remains,
still charged with our lives,
thick with our voices, spoken and silent.
I flourished here once,
then left, holding my heavy heart.
Now I visit not with regret,
but to honor what once was.

FOG

I wake up to fog. I pull the chord on the blinds and see that fog season has rolled in. I can't see very far at all, just the trees across the street, and then foggy trees, and then nothing but fog. I prefer a horizon. All the way out to the edge of the earth if possible. I prefer clarity to fogginess. I prefer green crisp leaves to a lumpy gray blob.

The fog protects the canyon from sun, protects the coyotes nursing their pups, the raccoons polishing their food in the creek, the rodents from the swoop of the owl.

The canyon is asleep under a batting of gray, a quilt of softness covers the budding tree boughs. The rough tree trunks hunker down for some time of quietude free from upper level tenants hopping about from limb to limb, and its bark freeway-runners exceeding speed limits.

Fog fills my need for settling in. Frees me from the pulse of the warm sun, endless days of bump and grind, nights of bad music. I long for a blanket to smolder the fire. I long for the wild chatter of the airwaves to be hushed. It has spiraled into a noise only dogs can hear.

Maybe a long fog season for the earth could squelch wars, or keep mothers home with their babies; maybe fog could spoil phone lines from planning destruction, or cause long-term color blindness, maybe keep the reservoirs from evaporating our life-saving liquid. It comes so quietly, like a cat in the night, so simply, like a tongue to salt. It's amebic shape wanders over latitude and longitude, into gullies and caves, under unkept promises and overdue looks.

I think the fog around me helps me to look in, remember how I got to here. Who will I still want in my fog-bank when all the dazzle is gone? Now I know why I didn't pass go, why I couldn't collect the money.

Rolling in a fog bank could be the next big feature at Disneyland. Going in with chaos attached; coming out with serenity, and perhaps a sense of purpose.

I let the window blind down again and go back to bed with a good book.

MY ORDINARY LIFE

The parrots came out to dry their feathers. I don't know where they go when it rains, but they make a lot of noise when they gather in my neighbor's tree again. My neighbors hate the squawking and mess on their chaise lounges. Sometimes they bring out a BB gun and shoot up into the tree, hoping the parrots move on to someone else's life.

My neighborhood hasn't been as noisy as this since the violinist lived across the street. He played in the symphony, so his violin playing was not to be scoffed at. And it wasn't the violin that was so noisy, it's just that he annoyed his wife so much it made her into a screaming maniac. We could hear her screaming at him, "You are drunk!, You are mean! I'm calling the police!" The screaming would end and I would see her come out of the house in her faded-pink, chenille robe and throw something into the garbage can with a thud. I think she just wanted the neighbors to see how angry she was. And we would see her, with her frizzy hair, worn slippers, and robe of almost no color, steaming angry and telling the world about it. When things settled down, he would bring a folding chair out to the driveway, take his violin out of its case, and play a few minutes of Beethoven or Brahms. Then he died of cirrhosis, and she sold the house and moved out. I miss the drama.

I'd miss the parrots, too, if they were to leave the neighborhood. It's like we need something to complain about in this ordinary place. Aside from the parade of well-groomed dogs being walked by dog walkers or owners, and a scramble of strollers, being pushed by nannies, or jogged behind by fathers with earphones, there isn't much going on. The green grass grows, the wind rarely blows, the garbage goes out on schedule. It is quite wonderful, this ordinary place, this ordinary time, this ordinary life.

Windows

THE PAINTINGS

Before I had children
I walked a corridor where paintings were hung.
Two of them struck me—
the first was a mother with four children pulling
at her skirt until it ripped into shreds.
The second was a woman in a tennis outfit,
sitting in her foyer
near the formal bouquet of flowers
on the French Provincial side board.
Her tennis outfit had become too tight.
Her racquet was sliding to the parquet floor.
She wore an expression of greater emptiness than
I'd ever imagined.
Now, I have four children
and have played tennis,
and I'm still riveted by the messages
of the paintings.

I OVERHEARD A SHAMAN

The plane was late,
the airport crowded,
the passengers struggled with baggage.
I took my place on the aisle—
24 D.

A little girl, maybe 3 years old,
blond pony tail and blue jeans,
sitting across from me
looked out the window.

We took off,
leveled out,
seats pushed back,
trays let down,
service carts rattled
down the aisle.

I heard her say:
"We're not on earth,
we're not in the sky.
I know, we're in heaven!"

Until then, I'd always wondered
where it was.

TWISTED SACRIFICE - 9/11

Pools of dark water sinking down
filled with a veil of tears falling
forever like a waterfall of grief.
Sheltered now with umbrellas
of golden leaves, dropping
condolences on the shoulders
of those reading the names.

Stunned voyeurs peer
at the one shoe, the keychain,
the burned wallet with family pictures.
Names are read aloud while we
gaze at their smiling faces, posed
on an ordinary day.

One remaining stairway witnessed
people escaping downward
with desperate feet,
while passing a boy in his fireman's uniform
sent up on a mission.
His eyes told them he knew
he was climbing
up the steps
to his death.

An escalator propelled us up
out of the crypt.
We passed the twisted steel beams
of the once-mighty building,
fused together, like giant hugs.
I felt the silent screams
of disbelief.

IN THE WRONG PLACE

Gourmet desserts were for special occasions
I no longer cared about.
I hadn't read the recipe until that morning.
After step one it said, "Let it stand overnight."
There was no overnight left.
Instead of the elegant chocolate mousse tart,
I would make-do with a pan of brownies.

The hands of the maître d' shook
when he checked us into the dining room.
We seemed alone, but there was a table set
across the room for twelve.

The old sheep barn, turned hotel,
was more strange than the language.
Making a two-day stay
with one special dinner
felt dangerous.

The table of twelve sang happy birthday
in English,
and then they stood and made a toast
to our national enemy.
What country were we in?

Not belonging anymore felt foreign,
but I had crossed a river
and could not go back.
I delivered the dessert, (substandard).
No glory here. No safety there.

THE WINDOW

The doors I closed
are behind me now.
But ring the buzzer of the dark door
on the stairway
closed in front of me
until I come out smiling,
and I am still there.

The door closed and locked
when all was past
and not a heartbeat of hope
could fill the vase with roses.

The door closed
to the warm air,
considering it better to freeze
than obey his lewd suggestion.

The place my mind lived was
in the blue box, I can still touch it,
the azure box, the cube of it,
the short cover, the wrinkle of tissue.

Inside the box was
Cinderella, dancing plastic dress,
safe with her plastic prince,
I could wind them up and the waltz
would take me out
through the bedroom window.

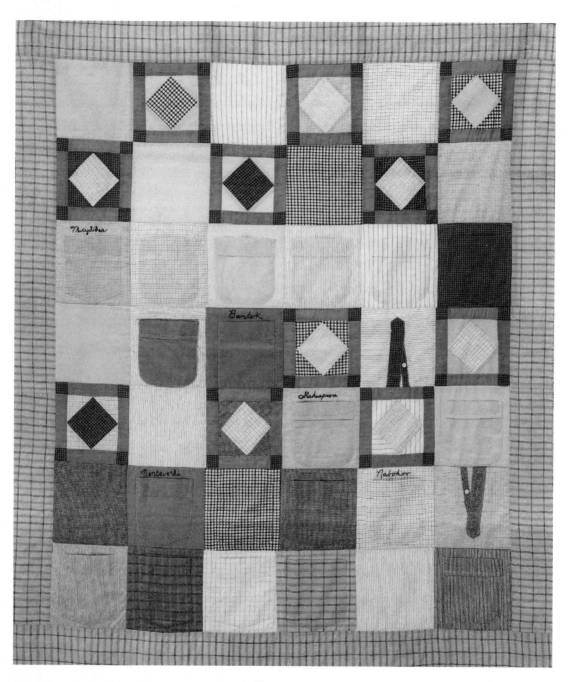

Favorites

BLOOD MOON

The blood moon hid from me
behind gauzy clouds.
How unfortunate.
The moon, nights before
and nights after,
was a white, glowing beacon,
round as a radish and
glowing like a bride.

Tonight, I caught the faint red rim
just below the white-ribbon cloud.
It was there for seconds, then gone,
and it didn't come back again.

There in silent language,
I find hidden stories.
Something is a secret,
a fatal flaw,
a human frailty.
Look quickly!

The moon is saying, "Look here, too.
See my embarrassments,
see my failures, my transgressions.
Could you love me anyway?"

Transparent flaws,
shining through
without makeup and false tresses,
show beauty that binds us.

I hated the moon for showing up
only in a good light.
But I love the moon

who dares to show me
her bloody underclothes.

FROM THE INSIDE

What truth speaks from the inside
without the noise of words.
                    –Louis Andriessen - *Mysteriën*

The French horns blare,
their bells to the sky.
Timpani thunders, tubas pout,
the bassoon gives its plaintive cry, while
the piccolo hovers like a humming bird.

Gathering in the usual room,
the women take their places,
stitching in hand,
yarn, good wool, needles—
they create wedding or baby gifts,
warm promises,
or just use up supplies.

Their stories elevate
from chipped hearts
through dry throats quiet for too long
alone in missions of spousal care.

While gathered among friends,
they create visible products
that won't have to be repeated
on the medicinal schedule.

With conversation
their concert continues:
he sleeps between doses,
she struggles to make the day ordinary,
the nutrients sit upon her shoulders,
heavy in delivery.

He thinks there are people talking
to him and she is not one but two
through the haze of medications
that may cure but never
make them whole.

In monotonous rehearsal at home,
caring overwhelms, exhausts,
pushes skills into tasks unthought of.

Still, a ribbon of promise lies
in looking ahead to the next
gathering with friends
where she can express her burden
and stitch herself together again.

LASTING STITCH

My home is death ready—
windows washed,
bathrooms clean,
dishes put away.
If I die on my way to the golf course,
(or the ski slope)
it would be a great way to go.

My home is in perfect shape—
plans for burial in upper right-hand drawer.
Will in file cabinet,
personal letter with it,
a foil, a camouflage for what there is hidden.

I am ready for no one to know what I left undone,
what I left unsaid, what I left hidden.
Look in the drawer in the studio,
under the fabrics,
behind the door, inside the toolshed,
under the refrigerator.
Look there. Look there.

Pieces of my selfish victories,
threads of my daydreams,
scraps of self-revelation,
mirrors of self-deception
and the core of my emotions
wrapped in fleece,
hidden to look like innocence.
This humanness comes oozing out of the corners.

Death makes saints out of men and women
who don't deserve it.
We grasp at threads of life.

Weavings of pretense hide failings of judgment,
lapses of conscience, oversights of duty.
We hear great men confessing, and our pride swells.
We read the obituaries, and revel.
We visit the care center, happy to wear a visitor's badge.

Fraying. Wafting in breezes. Shredding in time.
Peeling down to the core of who we are.
Pretense aside, aching with reality,
knowing deeply what folly we live in.
Hoping one good deed was done
to leave this world with a lasting stitch.

ELEGY FOR PEACHES N. CREAM

I wake with a wet, warm leg.
I jump up, but Peaches just raises her fuzzy head.
It's Sunday.
All last week I dealt with dog accidents.
So unusual since we installed the doggy door
several years ago.

Peaches, lately, would stand staring at a wall.
Peaches, lately, would not hear words like
"Go for a walk?" or "Are you hungry?"
or "Want a treat?"
Peaches lately would nap.
She would nap through the mailman
rattling the metal mailbox.
She would nap through pizza deliveries,
She would nap through squirrels and skunks
trespassing on her city lot.
And now she was sleeping through her incontinence.

I snapped her leash to her collar.
She made it down three steps.
Then she sat down.
Brown eyes looking up at me said, "Help."
She took three or four more steps,
then sat down and again looked up.
"Fix this."

On the drive to the 24-hour dog hospital,
she relaxed on my lap,
wrapped in her blanket.
While we waited for the vet, we remembered
how she never missed posing in a family photo,
the time she was sprayed by a skunk,
the way she would run in circles after her bath.

We shared her joy for 16 1/2 years.

I held her close to my heart and whispered,
"I love you, Peaches" in her ear
while the doctor injected
magic sleep-forever solution into her veins.
I held her limp body against my beating heart.
She was at peace, I was at peace.
When I die, I'm going to the vet.

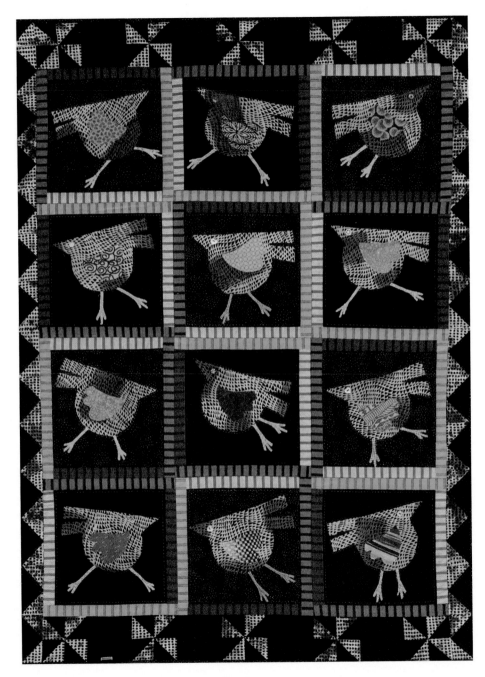

Fly Away

CHARLES

Charles Bukowski and I
have become good friends.
His name doesn't fit him,
it should be Alfred or
Frank, maybe even George.
But, either way, he has
bared his soul to me.

I get disgusted
with his womanizing,
but then...
I'm sorry to hear
about his gambling
on the horses,
but then...
His drinking to excess
didn't bother me so much,
don't know why.
He just loved that security
bottle of beer by his side.

I love that he wanted
to be an ice cream person,
and that under his tough skin,
he is really a bluebird.

I wouldn't let him
pick me up at the bar.
But if I could talk with him,
I'd have a lot of questions.

His outsider status
is most fascinating
because,

I am standing there too,
on the outside,
looking at the snow globe
of someone else's life.
Observing, recording,
without really knowing
until later, maybe,
what I have seen.

We just stand there,
Charles and I,
on the scaffolding
taking note
of the goings-on
as if it's a class play
in the gymnasium
of the elementary school,
on the corner.

CAN YOU HEAR ME NOW?

–After Charles Bukowski

Ask the wallpaper
Ask the kitchen sink
Ask the dog lying on the rug
Ask the happiest woman you can find
Ask the grandmother
Ask the woman with panic attacks
Ask the blind
Ask the pill taker
Ask the therapist
Ask the hairdresser
Ask the most miserable woman in her
    most miserable moment

Ask the woman on chemo
Ask Madame Currie
Ask Queen Elizabeth
Ask the woman who gathers eggs
Ask the woman who rocks the baby
Ask the school teacher
Ask the clerk at CVS stocking shelves
Ask a map of France
Ask Ann Landers
Ask Siri

Ask the landlady collecting rent
Ask the ladies who lunch on Tuesdays
Ask the fragrant lemon tree
Ask the church lady
Ask the drunk – sorry again
Ask the mother while she is giving birth
Ask the woman during a hot flash
Ask the women who read the New York Times

Ask the ones who sack groceries at Ralphs

Ask your Aunt Edna fluffing pillows in the parlor
Ask the Olympic champion receiving her medal
Ask the fat women, the anorexic, the body builder
Ask the ticket taker at a freak show

Ask any of these, or all of these
They, all of them know
Ask, ask, ask and they'll tell you:

A husband in the kitchen,
with his nose in the newspaper,
who pretends to listen, but doesn't,
is more than a woman can bear.

OM

I look inward to hear
with my spleen, my liver,
my missing appendix.
I listen through fog
or deep under water.
Find sunken songs,
wishbones and old china.
I want to hold my breath
or use yours to continue.

But now I breathe in time
to slowness that is out of the race,
to being that is effortless,
to just so, with a
long inhale, endless exhale.

In resistance of peace,
I splash along at the surface.
I feed off reflections
while the dream lies deep.

I have the red leash.
It's not the right leash,
it's not even the right dog.
So why am I buying dog food?

I let go of responsibility
and become part of a galaxy,
part of gravity.
I let go of self and who I think I am.
I float just low enough
to pass for normal.

A RISE IN TEMPERATURE

No one would believe me, or trust
that I wasn't making a big mistake
as I ran from minus 15 to 98 sizzling degrees.

I ran,
leaving zero population growth
and settled into one space in a can of sardines.

I ran
from a home with a view to a tiny room
where I could hear the man in the next building
spit into his toilet.

I ran
from plenty of juxtaposition but little relationship.

I ran
starving, crying out, like a newborn baby
with her first smell of mother's milk.

A spider's web had caught me,
stuck me to its net
while breezes tossed me into a new sensibility.
The handrail of God felt solid enough
for me to take the leap and perhaps
find one insect to nourish me along the way.

Looking for the fork in the road had come to an end.
Forty-four years of wandering in the wilderness was over.
I could no longer trust the deep water I was in
and I didn't want to keep paddling there
without my box of letters

and the wine cooler.

So I rode off on my trusty horse,
through fields of sunflowers and sugar beets,
black angus, fishing boats,
apple pie and ice cream.

Across the fruited plain, the purple mountains,
and into dry desert land I rode.
Even the neighbor's dog
didn't know where
I had gone.
But I was soon there in the choir loft
where a heart is safe
and a brain can start to sing its own melody.

And now, looking back, I see
my petri dish was waiting,
the ingredients were in my fingertips
all along.
The grocery cart that I had filled
and thought I had to push,
had turned itself upside down
and had started to churn out
a mango banana smoothie.

ALLIGATORS, BEAR CLAWS AND SNAKES, OH MY!

I hate going to the grocery store
because of all the snakes.
The hate, the dread, the slow, worried, sick feeling
begins early in the morning when I reach
for the almond milk and there is none.
I look at the list on the counter.
Someone has written peanut butter,
someone has written chips,
and 3A batteries.
I write down the basics:
milk, eggs, bacon,
orange juice, bread,
the will to cook,
the will to go to the grocery store,
the willingness to carry heavy
grocery bags to the car
and then into the house
and then into the pantry
and refrigerator.
The snakes are lurking in my mind
all this time,
ready to scare me right to death
and I don't know why they are there.
I don't know why they are in my purse,
and in my trunk where I keep the grocery bags,
and then in the aisles of the store,
perhaps behind the blue cheese
or the pasta.
I never know where they will peer
out at me.
I know they like the meat counter,
but they don't hang around the bakery—
they hate sugar.
So I take a number and stand in line

to choose a bear claw or alligator
(not at all frightening).
I pay and begin to pinch off pieces
from inside the white paper bag
while I continue to shop.
While tasting the almond paste
and pecan fillings I feel no fear of snakes,
I can't even remember
what snakes look like,
or why I hate them.

Perhaps if the baker could listen
to my idea of how to solve this dilemma,
my fear of snakes could be over.
Next time you are looking in
the bakery counter for something
to soothe your cravings,
choose the long donut with the
black and yellow diamonds,
or the curled up one next to
the elephant feet that has rust and brown
stripes along its back.
The alligator and bear claw won't be upset.
They are waiting for me.
I'll choose them.
But would you please do me a favor?
Eat up all the snakes.

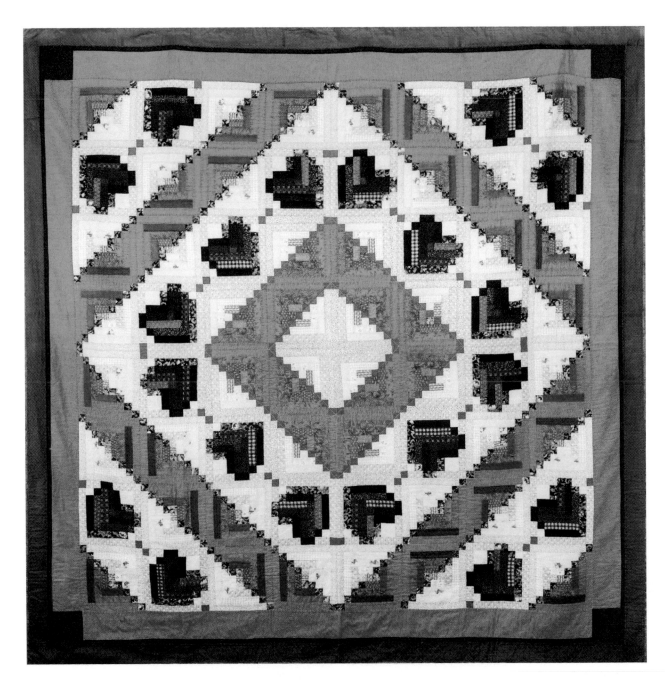

Looking For Lake Valentine

BEAT OF THE HEARTLAND

My view is of the parking lot
through my rain-spattered hotel window—
five pick-up trucks parked near my rental car—
macho yet practical.
Beyond are church steeples,
public TV antennas,
stores and hospitals I know well.
I keep coming back,
enjoy the memories,
look for warnings I missed before.

I travel the city streets, potholed
from winter's ice,
the country roads over-graveled,
tractors tossing dust in their wake.
I pass fields of sunflowers
bowing their heads
as I drive by in my rental car.
The lakes I knew wave to me.
The trees flutter their leaf lashes.
This mid-country state knows
my innocent love of it,
and it loves me back.

Fly-over-land is stable,
non-violent, with good-looking men,
strong women, bright children,
religious good will,
respect for work ethics,
and the certainty of the right way.
But geese honk above me—
warnings
I couldn't hear before.

I overhear "You betcha" and
"That's so precious" as I
sip my weak coffee at Gathering Grounds.
The food is too sweet and too cheesy.
The stores try too hard to make things cute.
People are all my aunts, cousins,
swimming-lesson buddies.
Men of all colors can be trusted,
at least that is my first reaction.

The fields of soy beans and
corn stalks, lush with promising viridian,
bask in sunshine until the hail comes,
or the drought.

My heart loves something here
and revels in the windy days,
the cloud-painted sunsets,
the black fertile earth.
Yet, there lurks in the cemeteries
and well-kept farm yards
a message to leave,
see more, live more.

But from my hotel window,
I watch the church-goers this Sunday
making their way with promises to remain
steadfast and unwavering.
Perhaps my strength comes from
growing up here, soaking the steadiness in,
feeling the beat of the heartland.

WINTER OF LOVE

I had memorized some of his moves
on the court and the scores
so I could sound like
I knew what was going on.

He held the heavy door open for me
at the rear exit of the high school.

His athletic jacket was unsnapped and the
smell of aftershave wafted into my nostrils.

My mind was on his 52 Plymouth
left running in the parking lot
so I would not be chilled sitting on the
fake leather upholstery.

I had perfected my blond pageboy,
worn my pencil skirt and matching shoes,
in spite of warnings from my mother
that I would slip on the ice.

I'd waited all week for this night, when we would drive off
to nowhere and he would turn the radio to the local
station so we could hear this week's top ten hits
played from ten down to one by midnight.

Here we were, alone at last
after the crowd had finished cheering
and the cars with their puffing exhaust pipes
were heading away.

Snowflakes were falling on our faces.
He looked up at the sky and beamed
like the light on a new Schwinn bicycle.

I thought it was the most romantic of moments,
and I wanted the night to last forever.
As he held the car door open for me he said,
 "I can't wait 'til tomorrow when I can go skiing!"

MORNING WALK AFTER EYE SURGERY

My dog pees on everyone's lawn,
sniffs each bush for news
as I walk her on
her pink leash.
My neighbor comes out
with stitches on her eyelids.
She needs to walk,
a break from her
wheelchair husband.

Nannies swing blonde babies
in the small park of plastic playthings.
They are on their iPhones
checking
on their abandoned children.

We get to the bluff and count
four sailboats,
six surfers.
Sharks we can see from above
can't be seen
from the beach.

All the way home we
talk of her surgery,
neighbors,
TV shows.
Back in the house
the dog eats her breakfast,
I read the Times,
put a jigger of Bailey's Cream
in my cold coffee.

PATRICK'S ROADHOUSE

Lizzy got a job as manager at Patrick's Roadhouse.
The building is painted shamrock-green.
A porch, of sorts, hides the front door.
Rusted signs with arrows pointing
to the beach, or some outdated
price of gas, are hanging on the wall
laced with hardy vines
that can hold up to the salt air.

The roof is quite flat, with large objets d'art
placed prominently on top: a green elephant,
a dancing leprechaun, a dinosaur.
You can spot them just beyond
the gas station as you
drive north on the PCH.

The OPEN sign is in the window
most hours of the day and night.
And patrons, like celebrities, come there
for breakfast and lunch, to make
or break deals, hide from public eye.

The night visitors are those
who walk the PCH at night to keep
safe, and sleep on the hillsides
when the sun can warm them.
They arrive dirty, penniless,
drunk and delusional,
order food like the rest of us.

Employees find it difficult
to stay focused with the smell,
the dirty clothing,
the mumbling and hallucinations.

Patrons who holler, urinate,
or simply don't pay are hard
on one's composure.
Two weeks on the night shift is an eternity.

Lizzy came to work there,
It was a job that fit her skills,
her caring heart
and her personal connection
with being a fish out of water.

First she helped the workers by showing them
how to care about each other and become a team.
Then she inspired them to see each person
as worthy of being heard and seen.

She would tell jokes, explaining that people
listen better when they are smiling.
She would invite the homeless to her house sometimes
for a shower and a nap, but have all traces
of them gone when her mother returned home at 5 p.m.

Lizzy loved her customers.
She took them into her heart:
their grief, hopelessness and brokenness.
She had no filter.
This became her life's work.
Her short life's work.
Her very short life's work.
Lizzy's mother found her on the floor
late one night.
She died of a broken heart at 35.

20-20 HINDSIGHT

There were three chairs already taken when I got to the small room to wait for my eyes to dilate. I could sit by the wall, or take the seat next to the very old man with the oxygen tank and walker. I took that one. He adjusted his walker so I could have more space. The oxygen tank on his walker was connected by plastic hosing to his nostrils. He sat quietly, curled into the letter C that old people seem to succumb to when their muscles no longer hold their bodies erect. His daughter was in one of the other chairs, reading a magazine.

I made some comments about the mist as I drove in, we had a short conversation about LA and rain. His daughter said, "I'm headed for the ladies room, Dad. I'll be right back." She left her car keys and cell phone on the small table between the chairs.

I liked his tweed sport coat, neatly pressed pants and rather-new shoes, if he could stand all the way up he may have been over six feet tall. He looked well-cared for and intelligent as he twisted sideways to see me next to him. He told me he had lived on the East coast, Washington D.C. and New Jersey. He was a corporate lawyer. We chatted a short while about being a lawyer and then the doctor called him into the examining room. He stood up slowly, gripping the walker handles with the oxygen tank attached. He projected ahead the five or six steps toward the open archway while the doctor waited. As he left, I said, "I enjoyed talking with you."

As my eyes were dilating, I tried to read my emails and play Words with Friends, but things got blurrier and I begin to complain with the other two people waiting how long the wait was getting to be. Then there were strange noises in the hall and uniformed people were rushing by. The regular sounds of the doctor's office were gone, the hushed hurry of emergency procedures took over. Almost an hour passed before one of us waiting-room captives was called to the examining room.

The daughter, who had been gone far too long for just a restroom visit, came in, grabbed her phone and keys and said, "Now I have everything," to someone in the hall. She left.

When I finally got in to see my doctor, he went through the usual blinding, bright-light evaluation and gave me the information regarding my future eyesight. He said, "Do you have any questions?" I said, "I just need to know if the emergency involved that nice old man I talked to in the waiting room." His answer was what I expected: "You know I'm not allowed to tell you that." His color changed and his eyes blinked as he looked at me. I said, "I know." I left the room wondering how that nice old man was, and that it WAS nice talking with him. I'm glad I told him.

MORNING IS BREAKING

I feel something warm and damp on my leg. I look at the clock: 6 a.m. I admit I am old, but I'm not yet incontinent. The dog!! She's the source of the warm and damp, now becoming wet. I pick her up, she opens her eyes like, "What's going on?" She has no idea. She is 16, I forgive her immediately and take her downstairs to the back door and put her down on the grass. Back upstairs I pull off the top sheet and the cotton blanket, which now have the odor of "Dog Pee Number One." My husband sleeps through it all, but now mumbles something about being cold.

I wonder if I will ever be alone? Will I ever be number one? Does any one remember, or care, that I was the one who jumped up to let the dog out, to hush the baby, to turn off the alarm, to wake the children, to fix the sandwiches, to shovel the walk, to warm the car, to be on time. Yes, I have driven them to school in my pajamas.

Will it ever just be me? Just me, the one in my bed? Just me without a baby to hear, a dog to let out, a lunch to fix, a hem to mend, or a meal to fix? Will I ever be the only one I'm caring for? (I really long for that sometimes.) I go back to bed, just for a little more shut-eye.

The phone rings. I groan as I reach for it.

I'm thinking, one morning I'll just roll over in my clean fluffy bed, the sun shining through my east-facing window, I'll hear birds in the trees and hear the neighbors start cars to go off to work. No dog will be begging for breakfast, or peeing on my leg. No husband checking for breaking news before he kisses me, no schedule to demand I jump out of bed. I'll lie there with my latest novel and some magazines, maybe the morning paper to inform me while I sip my coffee. My room is large, perhaps like one from *Downton Abbey,* papered and well-appointed. The servants bustle about, out of my ear shot. Still in my most diaphanous blue gown, I plan my day's costume in my mind. The small bell is on my table when I am ready to call for help in dressing. Once dressed, I stand in the doorway of my dream, with no idea of where to go, or what to do.

I pick up the phone. No one is there.

AAAAAAKKK! Thank God I woke up out of that nightmare! The coffee is perking, the green parrots are gathered in my neighbor's trees, enjoying their morning screeching. The dog needs help getting off the bed. Where are my yoga pants? I splash water on my face. "Please feed the dog!" I yell as I run out the door.

A LEASH OF YARN

In the yarn shop picking out the yarn,
making my choice, going by intuition,
I alone will be choosing—
whatever choice I make will be right.

Winding the yarn into a ball,
choosing the pattern,
selecting the needles,
finding a good place to sit,
listening to a book on tape,
creating a knitted something,
and perhaps a deadline
with someone in mind.

I knit to keep my hands busy
so I don't eat while watching TV,
don't fidget while attending a meeting,
or get nervous riding in the car
while in terrible traffic.

I feel purposeful, thoughtful,
farsighted, and responsible.
I can unravel and redo.
I can pull it all off and throw it away,
untangle and start again.
I control the stitches,
I control the needles,
I control my emotions,
and my tongue
far better than when I am not
on a leash of yarn.

Off leash, words flow out at random,
tangling emotions, breaking threads,

dropping stitches right and left.
Sometimes, before getting into all sorts of trouble,
I have to backstitch, even bite my tongue.

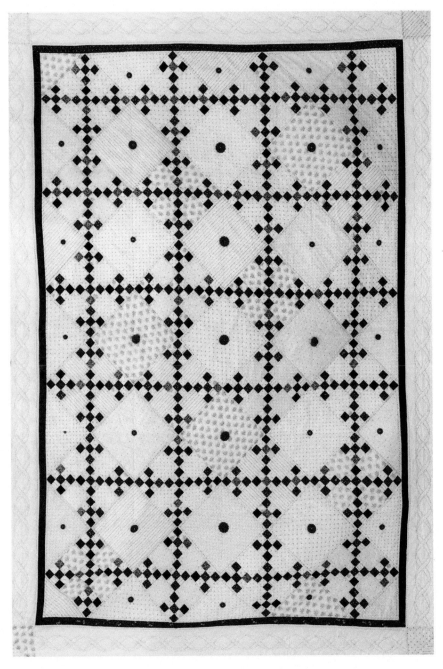

Kite Tails

BOY JUICE

Boy energy
comes through daylight like a locomotive,
steam pressure like Old Faithful
bursting forth on time.
Car handling becomes a fetish:
plugs, bearings, mufflers,
the manual on how to tame it
and call the signals.
Music sets forth on a roll down
a hill farther than the eye can see.
Lyrics lashing and licking their way
nourished by sudden angst
or joy that causes jumping.
Sharp blades cut ice while
black pucks hurl into nets.
Boy juice
fueling
boy batteries
launching space ships
to the back side
of Pluto.

THANKS FOR THE TALK

I'm working
I'm a writer
I'm working at my iPad
at the kitchen table.

I reach into my book bag,
find a crumpled paper,
it says: "Love doesn't
just sit there like a stone;
it has to be made like bread,
remade all the time,
made new."

I leave it in the bag.

Today I will edit
some work,
wash some clothes,
walk the dog,
make some appointments.

My grandson walks into
the kitchen, sleeping in
after a long night
writing music.
He puts bread into the toaster,
sits down at my table.

"Could I ask you some advice
based on your years
of wisdom?" he says
as he butters his toast.

I pretend to stroke my

long beard and
smoke my pipe.

Of course, it's about his
girlfriend of 2 1/2 years.
And about his going back
to school.
And about his need
for some freedom
to explore and experience
his career path
and relationships—
without being held back.

He talks, I listen.
I show him the quote
about how love
is like bread.
He says, "That's true."

He looks at his phone.
"I'm late for work!" he says.
He jumps up,
I wipe the crumbs off the table.
Five minutes later he
runs out the door.
"Thanks for the talk,"
he says.

HAPPY WITH MY SONG

I'm sitting here with my iPad.
I'm sitting here trying to become a poet.
I'm sitting here trying to have some genius thought
that arrives
out of the story of my day.

My teenage grandson comes
out of his room.
"I'm so happy with my song,"
he says.
"I'd like to hear it," I say.
"OK, let me do my hair
and then you can hear it," he says.

I walk barefoot across the hot patio
to his room behind
my garage.
It's a well-insulated room.
All the windows are closed.
He doesn't want his secret
music creations to get out.

I sit down on the arm
of the music-strewn couch.
There is no air to breath.
"I know it's stuffy," he says before I do.

He pushes one button on his computer.
Music blasts out like sudden thunder in a storm,
then becomes tender, peeking out from a
dark forest into light.
It builds with guitar layers, percussion.
His voice croons and cries,
and it all moves like waves crashing over rocks,

and then rafts down-river again.
I say, "I like it."
He says, "It has a lot of tonal dynamics."

I cross the hot patio and find
my glass of iced coffee,
now warmed from the sun.
I'm still sitting here with my iPad—
trying to be a poet.

KITE TAILS

I was sure they would turn out fine,
because I was blinded with love for them.
But I'm not sure if they are healthy;
I fed them SpaghettiO's
and a lot of ice cream.
I'm not sure they are honest;
I let them share their toys
and boundaries were soft.
I'm not sure they are accepting of others;
I sought out different shades
of skin for them to make friends.
I'm not sure they are hard workers;
we did the work together.
I'm not sure they are generous;
we had little, but it seemed enough.

I am sure they are just fine.
In spite of rough winds,
wickets, and hurdles along the way.

No one has won a Nobel Prize,
no one has made the headlines,
no one has made a million bucks
(but they always remembered my birthday).

I know they turned out just fine
because, although my love for them is still blind,
I let them go like kites into sky.
Now, I see trails of kite tails,
balancing the currents, high-spirited, lively—
sometimes tangled,
their kite tails dancing in the sun.

AN ALTAR IN THE WORLD

My neighborhood is quiet again—
clanking construction and dirt drifting
is past.
The new house next door is enormous,
ostentatious, taxes expensive,
blocking my view,
and home to a new family.

I'll adjust to the new.
But not forget the used-to-be
old house next door
with a TV antenna on the roof
and a dog barking through
the hole in the fence.
I'll not forget my small home
with my young children noising about.

My chubby-cheeked cherubs,
now grown, are coming home
all at once
from Switzerland, Colorado,
Washington, and Santa Monica.
Not so much to see me,
but to reunite with each other.
They are coming home
to free their child souls again.

 I'll be the one
eavesdropping to know
who's not getting along,
to find out what developments
they are not ready to tell me.
I'll be patching up the cracks
in relationships

when I can.

It is hard not to want it back—
sticky Valentines,
warm hugs that smell
like outdoors.
Although my tentacles
wrapped around them
once so tightly,
I've loosened up
over the years.

They make the pilgrimage:
fighting airports,
scrambling schedules,
dogs left in kennels,
children in tow.

They come back
to their first home
and their birth mother
who watches now
and listens.

I feel the moods vibrate
with guarded vulnerabilities.
I see old punches thrown
into new personalities.
I sense them slow
their pace
and voices,
learn again to trust
and lay their souls
at the altar of home.

TIME'S UP

Does time pass,
or do we pass through time?
Is time divine?
Are there timers in heaven,
or in hell, that chime?
Are angels or devils taking shifts
to implement the tasks
beckoned by the bells?
If I stood perfectly still for a long long time,
would I see a movie of history
on a screen
near my elbows?

The children gone, leaving palpable emptiness.
Apple sauce on a highchair tray,
smells of moist feather hair.
Wedding photos empty of experiences.
Hairdos with spray net safety.
Horseback lasses and dog whisperers.
Mud pies and baptisms for hollyhock dolls.
Lapping of lake water on my legs.

Remembering backwards
answers just some of the questions
concerning time.
It is humbling
to see how forces,
other than mine,
seem to have been in charge.
The teapot boils when I'm not watching.
The baby thrives,
the mirror lies at happiness.

The tightrope of concern
keeps me in fine balance.
Tension gathers in pillowcases
like plucked feathers
meant to fly off
with the breeze.

Chickens of Wisdom

With special thanks to Baz and Bambi and to Jack Grapes for all of
those chickens of wisdom he found at Ralphs.